vanishing from GRASSLANDS & Deserts

by Gail Radley

illustrations by Jean Sherlock

Featuring poems by Isak Dinesen, D. H. Lawrence, and others

Carolrhoda Books, Inc./Minneapolis

"Be infinitely tender and loving to animals." —'Abdu'l-Baha
For my dear friends the Neiheisels—Robin, Philip, Lauren, and especially Bill—because they care.
—G. R.

The status of animals can change over time. To find out about an animal's current status, you can check this website: **<http://endangered.fws.gov/wildlife.html#species>**. For animals outside the United States, click on Species Listed in Other Countries.

Photos in this book are used courtesy of: p. 4, © Tom Bean; p. 5, Gerald and Buff Corsi/Focus on Nature, Inc.

Text copyright © 2001 by Gail Radley
Illustrations copyright © 2001 by Jean Sherlock

This book is published in two editions:
Library binding by Carolrhoda Books, Inc.,
  a division of Lerner Publishing Group
Soft cover by First Avenue Editions,
  an imprint of Lerner Publishing Group
241 First Avenue North
Minneapolis, MN 55401 U.S.A.

Website address: www.lernerbooks.com

Words in **bold type** are explained in a glossary on page 30.

Library of Congress Cataloging-in-Publication Data

Radley, Gail.
  Grasslands and deserts / by Gail Radley; illustrations by Jean Sherlock.
    p. cm. — (Vanishing from)
  Includes index.
  Summary: Discusses through short essays and poems, ten endangered species that live in grasslands or deserts, including scientific information about each, reasons for its endangered status, and descriptions of efforts to protect it.
  ISBN 1-57505-406-X (lib. bdg. : alk. paper) ISBN 1-57505-568-6 (pbk. : alk paper)
  1. Grassland animals—Juvenile literature. 2. Desert animals—Juvenile literature.
3. Endangered species—Juvenile literature. [1. Grassland animals. 2. Desert animals. 3. Endangered species.] I. Sherlock, Jean, ill. II. Title. III. Series: Radley, Gail. Vanishing from.
QL115.3.R34 2001   97–28627
591.74—dc21

Manufactured in the United States of America
1 2 3 4 5 6 – JR – 06 05 04 03 02 01

Contents

Introduction

What would you do if the very last giant panda on earth was dying? You'd probably try to save it. Animals are dying out far more often than you might think. Scientists believe that about 50 **species,** or kinds, of animals die out each day. What's going on?

To understand, it might help to imagine all the pieces of a big jigsaw puzzle. Some pieces don't look important, and it's hard to see how they fit. But would you throw away those pieces? Of course not! You need them all to make a complete picture.

A giant elephant and a small white bird called a cattle egret help one another survive. The cattle egret eats insects on the elephant's skin. Besides grooming the elephant, the egret also acts as an alarm system, warning the elephant of approaching danger.

Our planet is a lot like a huge puzzle. The pieces come in different sizes. Some forms of life, such as bacteria, are very tiny. Others, like the mighty elephant or the towering redwood tree, are hard to miss.

Like puzzle pieces, all the living and nonliving things on the earth are connected. Some of the most important pieces of the puzzle combine to make up **habitats.** A habitat is the place where a plant or animal naturally lives. A habitat is made up of a mix of soil, air, water, weather, and living **organisms.**

The organisms in a habitat depend on each other to live. An **ecosystem** is the combination of organisms and their habitat. All ecosystems undergo change over time. Throughout history, changes in climate or habitat have made it more difficult for animals in an ecosystem to survive. When an ecosystem changes slowly, species have time to adapt. They can develop new traits to help them survive.

However, humans put many species in danger by making quicker changes to habitats. We cut down trees or grass so we can grow food or build houses. Humans also change environments by bringing in new plants and animals. The new species may compete with native species for food and space.

Humans use large amounts of natural resources. Water shortages and soil contamination change animal habitats. Hunting by humans has caused some species to die out and has pushed others in that direction. Laws to protect animals don't always help. Some animals have hides or other parts that are worth a lot of money. **Poachers**—people who hunt illegally—kill animals that are protected by law and sell their parts.

When the last member of an animal species dies, the species is **extinct.** Every animal that becomes extinct is a piece of the puzzle lost. And once that piece is gone, it's gone forever.

What's Being Done?

Scientists carefully watch animal populations. They call a species that's likely to become extinct **endangered.** **Threatened** creatures are not yet endangered, but their populations are shrinking. Some species fit into the **rare** category, meaning there have never been many of these creatures. A drop in a rare animal's population can push those creatures into the threatened group.

Ecologists make a recovery plan for animals in danger. They look at each creature's needs and think of ways to help meet those needs. Ecologists might suggest that lawmakers limit hunting of certain species. Sometimes scientists start a captive-breeding program. Wildlife experts capture threatened or endangered animals and take them to a zoo or a wildlife research center. Scientists hope the animals will be able to have babies and raise them in these safe places. If scientists believe the animals can survive in the wild, they may release some back into their natural habitat.

Scientists might recommend that land be set aside for a **wildlife refuge.** Here they maintain or restore habitats so that the land will support endangered, threatened, or rare creatures.

What Can You Do?

In *Grasslands & Deserts* you'll take a close look at 10 species in danger. As you read about these animals, think about how their stories make you feel. Do you feel sad? Or angry? Or happy that a species is doing better? A lot of people have written poems or essays to express their feelings about animals in danger. In this book, you will find a poem or other writing about each animal.

Reading about so many threatened animals can be overwhelming. You might think, "What could I possibly do that would make any difference?" Think again! Remember that big changes have to start somewhere. And they usually begin with small steps. To learn about what you can do to help, see the What You Can Do section on page 29.

UTAH
Prairie Dog

Prairie dogs look like sleek squirrels without the fluffy tails. They dig underground systems of tunnels, called burrows. In the burrows, which sometimes stretch for miles beneath dry grasslands, prairie dogs are safe from **predators.** Many kinds of prairie dogs live in the midwestern and western United States. But the Utah prairie dog is found only on the grasslands of Utah.

Utah prairie dogs share the grasslands with ranchers and cattle. The burrows that keep prairie dogs safe can cause cattle to trip and break their legs. Prairie dogs also eat the food that livestock need. So ranchers started to set out poisoned grain to kill prairie dogs. Between 1920 and 1972, the Utah prairie dog population dropped from about 95,000 to about 3,300. The federal government added Utah prairie dogs to the endangered species list. Utah passed laws against poisoning prairie dogs. The Utah prairie dog population increased to about 30,000. By 1984 the government was able to move the Utah prairie dog to the threatened list.

Prairie Dog

A prairie dog sits
straight up from his mound—
alert, like a soldier
he barks his alarm—
waking the weary,
warning the weak,
watching his family
flee from the eye
of the golden eagle.

Plump, furry prairie dogs
bolt back to their burrows
hiding in tunnels and rooms—
where prairie dogs play,
where prairie dogs sleep,
where prairie dogs nestle
and groom
their nursery of young,
safely tunneled beneath.

—Jill Morgan Hawkins

9

KEY *FACTS*

STATUS:
Endangered

SCIENTIFIC NAME:
Mustela nigripes

HISTORIC RANGE:
Western United
States and
Canada

SIZE:
18 to 24 inches
long; weighs
1 to 2 pounds

DIET:
Prairie dogs

LIFE SPAN:
12 years
(in captivity)

Black-footed Ferret

For a long time, scientists believed that black-footed ferrets, cousins of domestic ferrets, had completely died out. The animal's main food source had been the prairie dog. When ranchers began killing off prairie dogs, many black-footed ferrets starved, and others died from eating poisoned prairie dogs. Then a rancher's dog killed a strange-looking black-footed animal in Wyoming in 1981. Scientists identified the creature as a black-footed ferret.

In 1985 the Wyoming Game and Fish Department captured as many black-footed ferrets as they could find. Conservationists began a captive-breeding program. By 1991 the captive black-footed ferret population had increased from 18 to 200. Sadly, attempts to reintroduce the ferrets into their original habitat have failed. Most of the reintroduced ferrets have been killed by predators or by disease. Conservationists are doing their best to help the ferrets adjust to the wild. Until they do, the black-footed ferret's best chance of survival is in captivity.

Black-Footed Ferret

Ferret, friend of the Night
gently loping on the land;
black-banded button eyes,
burrowing and borrowing
warm tunnel-towns
from your sole, survival prey—
the prairie dog.
Sleek highwayman at dusk
hunting out your hideaway
in labyrinths of layered earth,
sly evader of the Day.

Silent seeker, searching
plains for frothy river streams,
in the land of the Sioux
and meadowlark—
standing upright as the Evergreen
as badger, bobcat and coyote call
beneath the amber Moon.

—**Jill Morgan Hawkins**

Galápagos Tortoise

KEY *FACTS*

STATUS:
Endangered

SCIENTIFIC NAME:
Geochelone nigra

HISTORIC RANGE:
Galápagos Islands

SIZE:
Shells 5 feet in diameter; weighs up to 550 pounds

DIET:
Ground vegetation and shrubs

LIFE SPAN:
Up to 200 years

Galápagos tortoises can weigh more than 500 pounds and live up to 200 years. Female tortoises have babies when they are 20 to 30 years old. They lay their eggs on the beach and cover them with sand. In 4 to 8 months, the eggs hatch. A month later, the babies dig their way out. Tortoises are most vulnerable to predators at this stage.

In the 1800s, European settlers came to the Galápagos Islands bringing goats, pigs, and dogs. These animals dug up tortoise eggs and killed young tortoises. By the early 1900s, 4 of the 14 giant Galápagos tortoise species were extinct.

In 1959 the government of Ecuador, which controls the islands, declared the Galápagos a national park. Conservationists set up a captive-breeding program to increase the numbers of the surviving species. The young tortoises develop in a protected environment and then are released into the wild. More than 14,000 tortoises now live on the islands. In 2001 an oil tanker spilled thousands of gallons of oil off the coast of the Galápagos. The tortoises were unharmed, but future oil spills may pose a threat to their habitat.

The Tortoise in Eternity

Within my house of patterned horn
I sleep in such a bed
As men may keep before they're born
And after they are dead.

Sticks and stones may break their bones,
And words may make them bleed;
There is not one of them who owns
An armour to his need.

Tougher than hide or lozenged bark,
Snow-storm and thunder proof,
And quick with sun, and thick with dark,
Is my darling roof.

Men's troubled dreams of death and birth
Pulse mother-o'-pearl to black;
I bear the rainbow bubble Earth
Square on my scornful back.

—Elinor Wylie

13

MHORR Gazelle

The word *gazelle* comes from an Arabic term that means "to be affectionate." Their long legs once carried Mhorr gazelles across the dry grasslands of Morocco in northern Africa. Mhorr gazelles can live without water for days, and they thrive in this harsh environment. But the animals have not been found in the wild since 1968. They are now found only in captivity.

Cattle ranching and other changes to habitat harmed the gazelle. But hunting was the biggest threat. Gazelle hunters particularly liked Mhorr gazelles. They are the biggest gazelle species, so they provided more meat. By the late 1800s, very few were left.

Hunting the Mhorr gazelle was outlawed in 1969. In 1971 a zoo in Spain started the first captive-breeding program for the gazelles. Other zoos have started these programs, too. The number of Mhorr gazelles in European and American zoos has grown from 17 to 200. Scientists hope to reintroduce the animal into its natural habitat in the future.

The Gazelle Calf

The gazelle calf, O my children,
goes behind its mother across the desert,
goes behind its mother on blithe bare foot
requiring no shoes, O my children!

—D. H. Lawrence

STATUS:
Endangered

SCIENTIFIC NAME:
Struthio camelus spatzi

HISTORIC RANGE:
Western Sahara Desert

SIZE:
Up to 8 feet tall; weighs up to 345 pounds

DIET:
Mostly green vegetation; occasionally eats lizards and insects

LIFE SPAN:
Up to 70 years (in captivity)

WEST AFRICAN
Ostrich

The West African ostrich can run as fast as 40 miles per hour! These birds zoom across the Sahara Desert in northwestern Africa. They are fast enough to outrun lions, leopards, and hyenas. But they are not fast enough to escape a hunter's bullet.

In the late 1800s, hunters killed vast numbers of West African ostriches. The hunters valued the birds' long, beautiful feathers, called plumes. The plumes were used to decorate hats and dresses. It looked as if the West African ostrich would disappear forever. Then ostrich farms sprang up to meet the demand for the plumes. People began to use ostrich skin to make wallets, handbags, and gloves.

Ostrich farming has probably been responsible for the survival of the species. With farm-raised ostriches available, hunters don't need to kill wild ostriches. Laws protect the wild ostriches from hunters. But loss of habitat continues to threaten West African ostriches. The plants, shrubs, fruits, and seeds that ostriches eat are not as plentiful as they once were. The West African ostrich is still in danger.

West African Ostrich

Sand and dust fly.
The ostrich runs.
Earthbound: feathers won't lift him,
Only mark him for the hunter,
the hatter.
The ostrich runs
On long strong legs.
He is vanishing . . . vanishing.
A swirl of dust in the desert.
A hissing roar.
A blink of dark fringed eyes,
And he is almost gone.

—Gail Radley

GELADA Baboon

Gelada baboons sleep on the rocky ledges above the grasslands of Ethiopia and Eritrea in eastern Africa. In the morning, Gelada baboons amble down into the meadows to eat grass, seeds, and roots. The baboons depend on this unique combination of high rocks and lower meadows. They cannot live anywhere else.

But this special habitat is disappearing. Farmers have planted crops in the Gelada baboon's habitat. As the grasslands vanish, the baboons have begun to eat the crops. Farmers defend their crops by killing baboons. Fur hunters shoot the baboons, too. A long, black mane covers the males' neck and shoulders. Native groups use this mane to make head-dresses and capes.

The Gelada baboon population continues to drop. The animal has been classified as threatened. Some baboons are protected from hunters in Semien Mountain National Park. But outside the park, it is still legal to kill baboons. Conservationists are trying to help the baboons before it is too late.

KEY FACTS

STATUS:
Threatened

SCIENTIFIC NAME:
*Theropithecus
gelada*

HISTORIC RANGE:
Ethiopia and
Eritrea

SIZE:
1½ to 2½ feet
tall; weighs up to
44 pounds

DIET:
Grasses, seeds,
leaves, insects,
fruits, and
vegetables

LIFE SPAN:
More than
20 years

From Baboon

. . . Thin-armed one with the thin hands
and smooth as a bullrush mat,
you walk along with arched neck.
Made light to be lifted up,
you swing yourself up into a tree . . . .

—a Khoisan tale,
  quoted by W. H. I. Bleek

KEY *FACTS*

STATUS:
Threatened

SCIENTIFIC NAME:
Equus grevyi

HISTORIC RANGE:
Ethiopia,
northern Kenya,
possibly Somalia

SIZE:
Up to 5 feet
4 inches tall at
the shoulder;
weighs up to
1,000 pounds

DIET:
Grass, shoots,
and leaves

LIFE SPAN:
Up to 25 years
(in captivity)

GREVY'S Zebra

The Grevy's zebra grazes in the dry scrubland of Ethiopia and Kenya in eastern Africa. At one time, Grevy's zebras could also be found in Somalia. But they have not been spotted there since 1973.

In the 1970s, hunters killed large numbers of Grevy's zebras for their uniquely striped skin. They sold the zebra skins to shoe and clothing makers. In 1976 the government of Kenya passed laws to try to save the zebras. They created two **preserves** to keep the animals safe.

But the Grevy's zebra's habitat is still threatened. Wars in Ethiopia and Kenya destroy the zebra's habitat. Tourists who visit the preserves trample and kill the grasses that the zebras eat. Hyenas, leopards, and lions hunt Grevy's zebras. Since 1987 the animal's wild population has dropped from 15,000 to less than 3,000. About 330 Grevy's zebras live in zoos and research centers. Captive-breeding programs may be the species' last hope for survival.

Zebra

The eagle's shadow runs across the plain,
Towards the distant, nameless, air-blue mountains.
But the shadows of the round young Zebra
Sit close between their delicate hoofs all day,
　　where they stand immovable,
And wait for the evening, wait to stretch out, blue,
Upon a plain, painted brick-red by the sunset,
And to wander to the water-hole.

—Isak Dinesen

21

KEY *FACTS*

STATUS:
Endangered

SCIENTIFIC NAME:
Petrogale xanthropus

HISTORIC RANGE:
Australia

SIZE:
About 2 feet tall; weighs 13 to 16 pounds

DIET:
Grass, bark, and roots

LIFE SPAN:
Up to 10 years

Wallabies are **marsupials** that live in Australia. Marsupials carry their young in pouches on their bellies. During the day, wallabies sleep in the coolest place they can find. At night, they hop around looking for food. Most wallabies are tan with very little other coloring. The yellow-footed rock wallaby is special. One of the smallest wallabies, this creature's coat is brown and pale yellow. Pale yellow stripes ring the yellow-footed rock wallaby's tail. No other wallaby has such unique coloring.

The yellow-footed rock wallaby's unusual fur has made it a target for humans. Hunters track down the animals and sell the fur to coat makers. In addition, the yellow-footed rock wallaby's habitat is shrinking. More and more humans are building ranches in the grasslands of northeastern Australia, where most yellow-footed rock wallabies live. Conservationists have preserved some of the wallaby's territory. Captive-breeding programs have also had some success. Nevertheless, the yellow-footed rock wallaby remains endangered.

From *Under the Range*

Where the gully shadows lie
Deeply blue before the sun,
In the shadow of the range
Wallaby are on the run. . . .

He makes his home that none will find,
The wallaby, the secret one,
Alone he runs his soakage pad,
Alone he sits when day is done.

Sits like a statue on the rocks,
His little striped face bright and wise,
And nothing stirs there that is not
Reflected in his eyes. . . .

—Irene Gough

NORTHERN HAIRY-NOSED Wombat

The northern hairy-nosed wombat uses its strong, curved claws to burrow beneath Australia's grasslands. The wombats spend their days underground, away from the hot sun. Sadly, the northern hairy-nosed wombat is the most endangered animal in Australia.

Since the late 1800s, ranchers have hunted northern hairy-nosed wombats. Digging wombats tear up fences and damage crops. Ranch animals sometimes fall into burrow openings and get hurt. Hairy-nosed wombats also compete with livestock for food.

The northern hairy-nosed wombat once lived throughout eastern Australia. These days the wombats can be found only in Epping Forest National Park in central Queensland. In 1971 only about 35 hairy-nosed wombats remained in the park. Conservationists banned hunting and barred cattle from the area. By 1995 the wombat population had increased to 80. Conservationists have started a captive-breeding program in Epping Forest. They hope to eventually reintroduce the animals to former habitats.

From *Weary Will*

The strongest creature for his size
But least equipped for combat
That dwells beneath Australian skies
Is Weary Will the Wombat.

He digs his homestead underground,
He's neither shrewd nor clever;
For kangaroos can leap and bound
But wombats dig for ever. . . .

—A. B. Paterson

25

Asiatic Lion

KEY FACTS

STATUS:
Endangered

SCIENTIFIC NAME:
Panthera leo persica

HISTORIC RANGE:
Turkey to India

SIZE:
About 6½ feet tall at the shoulder; over 8 feet long from head to body; weighs up to 550 pounds

DIET:
Medium- and large-sized plant-eating mammals

LIFE SPAN:
More than 15 years (in captivity)

Nature programs often show lions as aggressive animals that are constantly on the prowl for an animal. But lions actually spend most of their time—as much as 20 hours each day—sleeping. When they are awake, Asiatic lions hunt for deer or other large animals. They attack humans only when their habitat is threatened.

Asiatic lions once lived in grasslands from Turkey to India. But people have turned most of this area into grazing land for livestock in order to feed the growing population. The loss of habitat has caused the number of lions to drop. Asiatic lions have turned toward livestock, and even sometimes humans, for food. In the 1800s, people responded by poisoning lions. By 1908 only 13 Asiatic lions were living. The Indian government created a preserve in India's Gir Forest. Laws protect the species from harm. In the preserve, the number of wild lions has climbed to around 200. The mighty Asiatic lion is slowly recovering, but it still needs protection.

From *Lion*

The lion, ruler over all the beasts,
Triumphant moves upon the grassy plain
With sun like gold upon his tawny brow
And dew like silver on his shaggy mane.

Into himself he draws the rolling thunder,
Beneath his flinty paw great boulders quake;
He will dispatch the mouse to burrow under,
The little deer to shiver in the brake. . . .

He gazes down into the quiet river,
Parting the green bulrushes to behold
A sunflower-crown of amethyst and silver,
A royal coat of brushed and beaten gold.

—William Jay Smith

Map of Animal Ranges

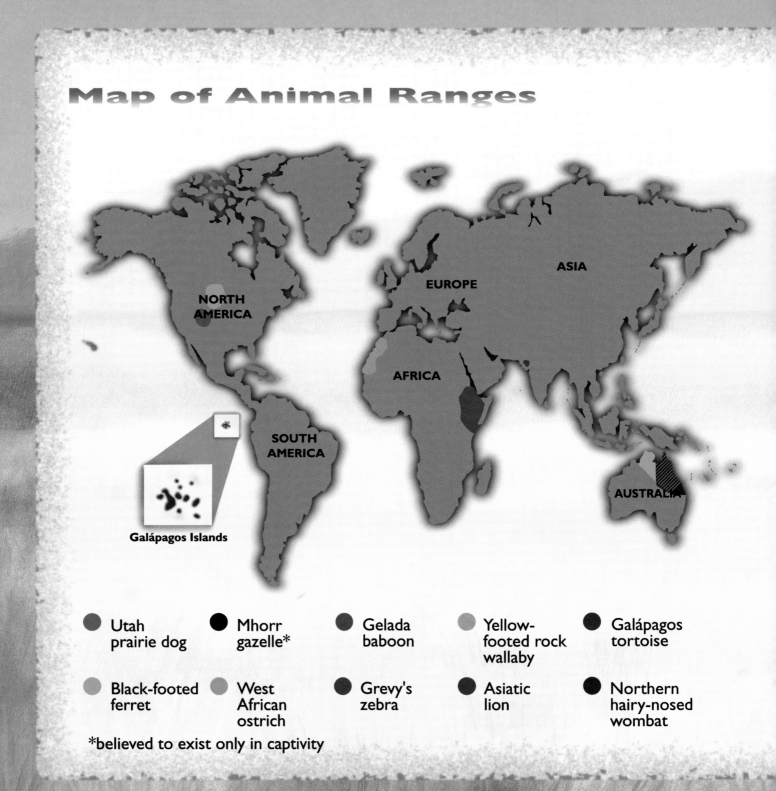

Galápagos Islands

● Utah prairie dog

● Mhorr gazelle*

● Gelada baboon

● Yellow-footed rock wallaby

● Galápagos tortoise

● Black-footed ferret

● West African ostrich

● Grevy's zebra

● Asiatic lion

● Northern hairy-nosed wombat

*believed to exist only in captivity

What You Can Do

The problem of species in danger may seem too big to tackle. But the efforts of many concerned people have saved some creatures from extinction. There are lots of things that young people can do to help.

Educate yourself.

- *Read books, nature magazines, and newspaper articles to learn about the animals. Then share your knowledge. When you spread the word about an animal in danger, you'll find that other people may want to help.*

- *Discuss a book about endangered animals for your next book report.*

- *Create a class scrapbook with pictures of each student's favorite endangered species.*

- *Create a save-the-animals bulletin board at school.*

- *Make informative buttons to wear on clothes or backpacks.*

- *Ask your teacher to arrange for a local conservationist to talk to your class.*

Take action.

- *Join a conservation club. People in these groups work to educate the public about endangered animals and their habitats.*

- *Encourage people not to buy products made from wild animal parts.*

- *When your parents are buying furniture or other products, ask if they'll shop around until they find ecosystem-friendly items.*

Help animals before they become threatened or endangered.

- *Set up a feeder for migratory birds.*

- *Help reduce air pollution—bike, walk, bus, or carpool.*

- *Pitch in on local clean-up days and encourage people not to litter.*

Decrease the amount of garbage your family or school produces.

- *Recycle glass, metal, paper, and plastic.*

- *Buy products made from recycled materials and shop at secondhand stores.*

- *"Precycle"—buy products that use the least packaging, such as food in bulk bins.*

For More Information

The following organizations have more tips on what you can do to help endangered wildlife:

National Audubon Society, 700 Broadway • New York, NY 10003 www.audubon.org

National Wildlife Federation, 8925 Leesburg Pike • Vienna, VA 22184 www.nwf.org

Sierra Club, 85 Second Street, Second Floor • San Francisco, CA 94105 www.sierraclub.org

World Wildlife Fund/Conservation Foundation, Education Department • 1250 24th Street NW • Washington, D.C. 20037 www.worldwildlife.org

Glossary

ecosystem: a carefully balanced community of soil, air, water, climate, and organisms

endangered: a category used by conservationists to describe species that are in danger of becoming extinct and that are unlikely to survive if present conditions continue

extinct: no longer existing

habitat: the place or environment where a plant or animal naturally lives

marsupial: a kind of animal that carries its babies in a pouch on the female's body

organism: any living thing

poacher: a person who illegally hunts wildlife

predator: an animal that hunts and eats other animals

preserve: land set aside for the preservation of an animal or plant species

rare: a category used by conservationists to describe species with small but stable populations that require careful watch

species: the basic groups into which scientists classify animals. Animals in the same species share traits that make them different from all other life-forms.

threatened: a category used by conservationists to describe species that are in danger of becoming extinct, but to a lesser degree than those that are described as endangered

wildlife refuge: land set aside as a shelter where wildlife can safely live

Further Reading

Cerfolli, Fulvio. *Adapting to the Environment.* Austin, TX: Raintree Steck-Vaughn, 1999.

Harrison, Michael, and Christopher Stuart-Clark. *Oxford Book of Animal Poems.* New York: Oxford University Press, 1992.

Hoff, Mary, and Mary M. Rodgers. *Life on Land.* Minneapolis: Lerner Publications Company, 1992.

Johnson, Rebecca L. *A Walk in the Desert.* Minneapolis: Carolrhoda Books, 2001.

Johnson, Rebecca L. *A Walk in the Prairie.* Minneapolis: Carolrhoda Books, 2001.

Patent, Dorothy Hinshaw. *Back to the Wild.* San Diego: Gulliver Books, 1997.

Relf, Patricia. *Magic School Bus Hops Home: A Book about Animal Habitats.* New York: Scholastic, 1995.

Vergoth, Karin, and Christopher Lampton. *Endangered Species.* Rev. ed. New York: Franklin Watts, 1999.

Index
Numbers in **bold** refer to illustrations

About the Author and Illustrator

Gail Radley has published nearly two dozen books. An animal lover, she's concerned about the large number of species whose survival is in danger. Radley lives with her husband, Joe, daughter, Jana, and their schnauzer, Toby, in DeLand, Florida. She is a lecturer in the English department at Stetson University.

Illustrator Jean Sherlock has long been combining her love of wildlife and her artistic talents. Her nature illustrations first appeared in publications while she was still in her early teens. When Jean isn't behind her easel, her interests include fishing, bird-watching, and above all, falconry. She and her red-tailed hawk enjoy hunting excursions throughout the United States.

Poetry Acknowledgments

The poems included in *Grasslands & Deserts* are reprinted with the permission of the following: p. 9, "Prairie Dog" Printed by permission of Jill Morgan Hawkins; p. 11, "Black-Footed Ferret" Printed by permission of Jill Morgan Hawkins; p. 13, "The Tortoise in Eternity" From *Collected Poems* by Elinor Wylie. Copyright © 1921 by Alfred A. Knopf, Inc. and renewed 1959 by William Rose Benet. Reprinted by permission of the publisher; p. 15, "The Gazelle Calf" by D. H. Lawrence, from *The Complete Poems of D. H. Lawrence* by D. H. Lawrence, edited by V. de Sola Pinto and F. W. Roberts. Copyright © 1964, 1971 by Angelo Ravagli and C. M. Weekley, Executors of the Estate of Freida Lawrence Ravagli. Used by permission of Viking Penguin, a division of Penguin Books USA; p. 17, "West African Ostrich" by Gail Radley; p. 19, excerpted from "Baboon" (in the public domain) quoted by W. H. I. Bleek in *Hottentot Fables and Tales*; p. 21, "Zebra" From *Out of Africa* by Isak Dinesen. Random House, Inc.; p. 23, excerpted from "Under the Range" The author has made every effort to obtain permission to use this excerpt from "Under the Range" by Irene Gough; p. 25, excerpted from "Weary Will" The author has made every effort to obtain permission to use this excerpt from "Weary Will" by A. B. Paterson; p. 27, excerpted from "Lion," by William Jay Smith. Copyright © 1956. Reprinted by permission of Harriet Wasserman Literary Agency.